JSON B

Easy Learning of JavaScript Standard Object Notation

By Steven Keller

Table of Contents

Disclaimer

While all attempts have been made to verify the information provided in this book, the author does assume any responsibility for errors, omissions, or contrary interpretations of the subject matter contained within. The information provided in this book is for educational and entertainment purposes only. The reader is responsible for his or her own actions and the author does not accept any responsibilities for any liabilities or damages, real or perceived, resulting from the use of this information.

The trademarks that are used are without any consent, and the publication of the trademark is without permission or backing by the trademark owner. All trademarks and brands within this book are for clarifying purposes only and are the owned by the owners themselves, not affiliated with this document. **

Introduction

JavaScript Standard Object Notation is used as a standard for the displaying of web pages on a web browser. This is of great importance to any programmer, and especially web developers. It is good for us to know how to use this. We should also know how to do conversions from other forms of data representation to JSON and vice versa. This book guides you on this. Enjoy reading!

Chapter 1- Conversions in JSON

JSON is widely used for reading data from a particular web server, and this data is then displayed on a web page. We can show how this is done by use of a string as the input.

String to Object

Create the string given below. Note that JSON syntax has been used:

```
var myString = '{ "students" : [' +
'{ "firstName":"Paul" , "lastName":"John" },' +
'{ "firstName":"Mercy" , "lastName":"Joel" },' +
'{ "firstName":"Peter" , "lastName":"Titus" } ]}';
```

The JSON syntax should be seen as a subset of the syntax used in JavaScript.

If we need to convert some JSON text into a JavaScript text, we use the "JSON.parse()" which is a JavaScript function. This takes the syntax given below:

```
var object = JSON.parse(text);
```

The newly created JavaScript object can then be used on a web page. This is shown below:

```
<p id="sample"></p>

<script>
document.getElementById("sample").innerHTML =
object.students[1].firstName + " " +
object.students[1].lastName;
</script>
```

When the above JavaScript code is combined with HTML for display on a web page, we should have the following:

```
<!DOCTYPE html>

<html>

<body>


<h2>Creating an Object from some JSON String</h2>


<p id="sample"></p>


<script>

var text = '{"students":[' +

'{"firstName":"Paul","lastName":"John" },' +

'{"firstName":"Mercy","lastName":"Joel" },' +

'{"firstName":"Peter","lastName":"Titus" }]}';


object = JSON.parse(text);

document.getElementById("sample").innerHTML =

object.students[1].firstName + " " + object.students[1].lastName;

</script>
```

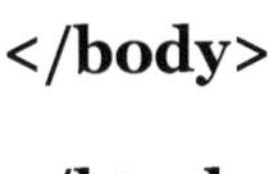

```
</body>

</html>
```

Once you open the above code in your browser, you will get the following output:

Creating an Object from some JSON String

Mercy Joel

The eval() function

In older browsers, the JavaScript JSON.parse() function is not supported. In such a case, we can use the eval() function so as to convert our JSON text into a JavaScript string. This takes the following syntax:

```
var object = eval ("(" + text + ")");
```

To open it on a web page, you have to combine it with HTML as shown in the code given below:

```
<!DOCTYPE html>
<html>
<body>
<h2>Creating an Object from a JSON String</h2>

<p id="sample"></p>
```

```
<script>

var txt = '{"students":[' +

'{"firstName":"John","lastName":"Paul" },' +

'{"firstName":"Mercy","lastName":"Joel" },' +

'{"firstName":"Peter","lastName":"Titus" }]}';


var object = eval ("(" + txt + ")");


document.getElementById("sample").innerHTML =

object.students[1].firstName + " " +
object.students[1].lastName;

</script>


</body>

</html>
```

Once you open the above in a web browser, you will get the following output:

Note that the student names have been stored in an array. We have then used that to get both the first Name and the last Name of the student stored at index 1, and that is Mercy Joel. Note that array elements start at index 0, and the index 1 denotes the second element in the array.

Conversions in Java and JSON

A tool named Google GSON can help us to convert our Java objects into the corresponding JSON format. Also, the vice versa is true, as the tool can be used when we need to convert our JSON format into the corresponding Java object. Although there are numerous tools which can be used for this conversion in Java, Google GSON is the best, as we are not expected to have a pre-annotated Java class or any Java source code classes.

The Java classes which do not support Generics are also supported in GSON. Let us demonstrate how this tool can be used:

We should begin by creating a class which we will be using in this section. The class should have the following code:

public class Student

```
{
  private Integer id;
  private String firstName;
  private String lastName;
  private List<String> permissions;

  public Student(){
  }

  public Student(Integer id, String firstName, String lastName, Date birthDate){
    this.id = id;
    this.firstName = firstName;
    this.lastName = lastName;
  }

  public Integer getId()
  {
    return id;
  }
```

```
public void setId(Integer id)
{
  this.id = id;
}
public String getFirstName()
{
  return firstName;
}
public void setFirstName(String firstName)
{
  this.firstName = firstName;
}
public String getLastName()
{
  return lastName;
}
public void setLastName(String lastName)
{
  this.lastName = lastName;
}
```

```
  public List<String> getPermissions()
  {
    return permissions;
  }
  public void setPermissions(List<String> roles)
  {
    this.permissions = permissions;
  }

  @Override
  public String toString()
  {
    return "Student [id=" + id + ", firstName=" +
firstName + ", " +
        "lastName=" + lastName + ", permissions=" +
permissions + "]";
  }
}
```

Note that we have created a Java class named "Student." The student has attributes, which include the id, the first and last names, as well as permissions. We have also created functions which will be used for getting each of these parameters as well as functions for returning the result of this.

There are two ways how Gson objects can be created. In the first way, it is possible for you to get a Gson object easily for purposes of faster coding, and in the second way, we make use of the GsonBuilder so as to create a Gson object which is a bit sophisticated.

The following code shows how we can make use of of these methods so as to create a Gson object:

//First way for creation of a Gson object for purpose of faster coding

Gson gson = new Gson();

//Second way for creation of a Gson object by use of GsonBuilder

```
Gson gson = new GsonBuilder()
        .disableHtmlEscaping()
        .setFieldNamingPolicy(FieldNamingPolicy.UP
PER_CAMEL_CASE)
        .setPrettyPrinting()
        .serializeNulls()
        .create();
```

As shown in the above code, in the first method, we have just created an instance of the Gson so as to create a Gson object and this has been given the name “gson.” That is the easiest way that one can create a Gson object.

In the second way, we have created an instance of GsonBuilder. This object has been given the name "gson." Note that the "new" keyword has been used for instantiating the GsonBuilder. The object which results, that is, gson, will be of the type GsonBuilder. The good thing with this method is that there are a number of options which one can specify, and these will be applied to the object in question.

Conversion from Java to JSON

In Java, we use the toJson() function when we need to convert our Java object into JSON format. The following code demonstrates how this can be done:

```
Employee student = new Student();

student.setId(1);

student.setFirstName("John");

student.setLastName("Paul");

student.setPermissions(Arrays.asList("STUDENT",
"MEMBER"));

Gson gson = new Gson();


System.out.println(gson.toJson(student));
```

Output:

{"id":1,"firstName":"John","lastName":"Paul","roles
":["STUDENT","MEMBER"]}

Note that in the above example, we began by creating an instance of the Student class. We have named this “student”. This instance has then been used for setting both the firstName and the lastName of the student. The firstName has been set to John, while the secondName has been set to Paul. Note that the student was given an id of 1.

The student has also been assigned permissions. This has been done by use of the “setPermissions()” method which we created earlier on. The student has been granted two permissions, that is, STUDENT and MEMBER permissions. These should specify the kind of activity they can perform.

JSON to Java

It is also possible for us to convert the JSON format into a Java object. This is done by use of the "fromJson()" method. The following code demonstrated how this can be done:

```
Gson gson = new Gson();

System.out.println(
   gson.fromJson("{'id':1,'firstName':'John','lastName
':'Paul','roles':['STUDENT','MEMBER']}",
   Student.class));
```

Output:

```
Student [id=1, firstName=John, lastName=Paul,
roles=[STUDENT, MEMBER]]
```

Note that, as shown in the above example, the student details have been passed in the "fromJson()" method. These were then converted into a Java object, and that is why you can see the output shown above.

Creation of an Instance Creator

The Gson library can be used for creation of instance creators even if the class does not provide us with a default no-args constructor. However, you may sometimes find problems with such classes. In such a case, you can make use of the InstanceCreator so as to solve the problem. The InstanceCreator of a particular type of a Java class should first be registered with the Gson before we can begin to use them.

Consider the class given below in which we have no default constructor:

public class Club

```
{
  public Club(String clubName)
  {
    this. clubName = clubName;
  }

  private String clubName;

  public String getClubName()
  {
    return clubName;
  }

  public void setClubName(String clubName)
  {
    this. clubName = clubName;
  }

  @Override
  public String toString()
```

```
  {
    return "Club [clubName ="+ clubName +"]";
  }
}
```

In the following example, you will see how the Student class is referencing the “Club” class. This is shown below:

```
public class Student
{
  private Integer id;
  private String firstName;
  private String lastName;
  private List<String> permissions;
  private Club club; //Club reference

  //The setters and getters
}
```

For the class “Club” to be used in the correct manner, the InstanceCreator has to be registered for the Club.java class. This is shown below:

```
class ClubInstanceCreator implements InstanceCreator<Club> {

  public Club createInstance(Type type)

  {

    return new Club ("None");

  }

}


/* <strong>the InstanceCreatorgiven above should be used as shown below</strong>*/


GsonBuilder gsonBuilder = new GsonBuilder();

gsonBuilder.registerTypeAdapter(Club.class, new ClubInstanceCreator());

Gson gson = gsonBuilder.create();


System.out.println(
```

```
gson.fromJson("{'id':1,'firstName':'John','lastName':'Paul','roles':['STUDENT','MEMBER'],'club':{'clubName':'Music'}}",
        Student.class));
```

Output:

```
Student [id=1, firstName=John, lastName=Paul, roles=[STUDENT, MEMBER], club=Club [clubName=Music]]
```

In most cases, our aim is to write or read the JSON values which are not a default representation of the Java object. This calls for us to write a Java serializer and desrializer which is of that Java type. Let us demonstrate this by writing a custom serializer of the "java.util.Date" Java class. With this, we will be in a position to write the date in the "DD/MM/YYYY" format.

The code for the class Dateserializer.java should be as follows:

```
import java.text.SimpleDateFormat;
import com.google.gson.JsonPrimitive;
```

```
import java.lang.reflect.Type;

import java.util.Date;


import com.google.gson.JsonSerializationContext;

import com.google.gson.JsonElement;

import com.google.gson.JsonSerializer;


public class DateSerializer implements
JsonSerializer<Date>
{

  private static final SimpleDateFormat dtFormat =
new SimpleDateFormat("dd/MM/yyyy");

  public JsonElement serialize(Date date, Type
typeOfSrc, JsonSerializationContext context)

  {

    return new
JsonPrimitive(dtFormat.format(date));

  }

}
```

The following should be the code for the class "DateDeserializer.java":

```
import java.text.ParseException;

import java.text.SimpleDateFormat;

import com.google.gson.JsonDeserializationContext;

import java.lang.reflect.Type;

import com.google.gson.JsonDeserializer;

import com.google.gson.JsonElement;


import java.util.Date;

public class DateDeserializer implements
JsonDeserializer<Date>

{

  private static final SimpleDateFormat dtFormat =
new SimpleDateFormat("dd/MM/yyyy");

  public Date deserialize(JsonElement dateStr, Type
typeOfSrc, JsonDeserializationContext context)

  {

    try

    {

      return dtFormat.parse(dateStr.getAsString());

    }

    catch (ParseException ex)
```

```
    {
      ex.printStackTrace();
    }
    return null;
  }
}
```

At this point, you can make use of the "GsonBuilder" so as to register both the serializer and the deserializer. This is shown in the code given below:

```
GsonBuilder gsonBuilder = new GsonBuilder();
gsonBuilder.registerTypeAdapter(Date.class, new DateSerializer());
gsonBuilder.registerTypeAdapter(Date.class, new DateDeserializer());
```

The complete serializer and deserializer should be as shown below:

```
Student student = new Student();
```

```
student.setId(1);

student.setFirstName("John");

student.setLastName("Paul");

student.setRoles(Arrays.asList("STUDENT",

"MEMBER"));

student.setBirthDate(new Date());


GsonBuilder gsonBuilder = new GsonBuilder();

gsonBuilder.registerTypeAdapter(Date.class, new
DateSerializer());

gsonBuilder.registerTypeAdapter(Date.class, new
DateDeserializer());

Gson gson = gsonBuilder.create();


//Converting to JSON

System.out.println(gson.toJson(employee));


//Converting to java objects

System.out.println(gson.fromJson("{'id':1,'firstName
':'John','lastName':'Paul','roles':['ADMIN','MANAGE
R'],'birthDate':'25/09/2016'}"

                    , Student.class));
```

Output:

{"id":1,"firstName":"John","lastName":"Paul","roles":["STUDENT","MEMBER"],"birthDate":"25/09/2016"}

Student [id=1, firstName=John, lastName=Paul, roles=[STUDENT, MEMBER], birthDate=Jun 13 00:00:00 IST 2016]

The format we get from Gson by default is not very pretty and appealing to the eye. It comes in a compact JSON format, and the output JSON structure will have no white spaces. If we need to get a more amazing output, we should add the method "setPrettyPrinting()" to the GsonBuilder. This is shown in the code given below:

```
Gson gson = new GsonBuilder().setPrettyPrinting().create();

String jsonOutput = gson.toJson(student);
```

Output:

```
{
 "id": 1,
 "firstName": "John",
 "lastName": "Paul",
 "roles": [
  "STUDENT",
  "MEMBER"
 ],
 "birthDate": "25/09/2016"
}
```

Notice how the "setPrettyPrinting()" property has been set in the first line of the code in which we have the GsonBuilder() method.

Versioning Support

This feature is of great importance, especially in cases where you have the class file being modified in different versions. The fields of the class might also have been annotated with @Since. In this case, the file needs to be versioned. This can be done by use of the setVersion() method of the GsonBuilder. The following code demonstrates how this can be used:

```
GsonBuilder gsonBuilder = new GsonBuilder();

gsonBuilder.registerTypeAdapter(Date.class, new
DateSerializer());

gsonBuilder.registerTypeAdapter(Date.class, new
DateDeserializer());

//The version should be specified as follows

gsonBuilder.setVersion(1.0);

Gson gson = gsonBuilder.create();
```

The fields in the class Student.java should be added in various versions as shown below:

```
public class Student
{
  @Since(1.0)
  private Integer id;
  private String firstName;
  private String lastName;

  @Since(1.1)
  private List<String> permissions;

  @Since(1.2)
  private Date birthDate;

  //Setters and Getters
}
```

Now that the versioning feature has been added, we can test it as shown below:

```
//Use the version 1.0 fields
gsonBuilder.setVersion(1.0);

Output:
{"id":1,"firstName":"John","lastName":"Paul"}

/////////////////////////////////////////////////////////////
///

//Use the version 1.1 fields
gsonBuilder.setVersion(1.1);

Output:
{"id":1,"firstName":"John","lastName":"Paul","roles
":["STUDENT","MEMBER"]}

/////////////////////////////////////////////////////////////
///

//Use version 1.2 fields
```

```
gsonBuilder.setVersion(1.2);
```

Output:

```
{"id":1,"firstName":"John","lastName":"Paul","roles
":["STUDENT","MEMBER"],"birthDate":"25/09/2016
"}
```

That is how we can work around both Java and JSON objects.

JSON and ES6 Maps

In some cases, you may have some key-value data, but you may not know the keys for this in advance. These should be stored in an ES6 map rather than doing it in an object. However, most people find it hard to convert the ES6 maps to JSON and vice versa.

The map may have some arbitrary data. It can be encoded just like an array of key-value pairs, and this will help convert it into JSON.

If you need to convert your map into an array of pairs, you can make use of the spread operator. The following code demonstrates how this can be done:

```
let ourMap = new Map().set(true, 7).set({foo: 3},
['xyz']);
  > [...ourMap]
  [ [ true, 7 ], [ { foo: 3 }, [ 'xyz' ] ] ]
```

In case you have an array of pairs, you can make use of the "Map" constructor so as to convert it to a Map. This is shown below:

```
  > new Map([[true, 7], [{sample: 3}, ['xyz']]])
  Map {true => 7, Object {sample: 3} => ['xyz']}
```

The above knowledge can then be used when we need to convert a map which has some JSON-compatible data into JSON. The vice-versa is also true. This is shown below:

```
function mapToJson(map) {
  return JSON.stringify([...map]);
}
function jsonToMap(jsonStr) {
  return new Map(JSON.parse(jsonStr));
}
```

The functions can be used as shown below:

```
> let ourMap = new Map().set(true, 7).set({sample:
3}, ['xyz']);
> mapToJson(ourMap)
'[[true,7],[{"sample":3},["xyz"]]]'
> jsonToMap('[[true,7],[{"xyz":3},["xyz"]]]')
Map {true => 7, Object {sample: 3} => ['xyz']}
```

If your Map has only strings as the keys, it has to be encoded as an object so as to be converted into JSON.

In the functions given below, we are demonstrating how string maps can be converted to and from objects. Here is the code for this:

```
function stringMapToObject(strMap) {
  let object = Object.create(null);
  for (let [k,v] of strMap) {
    // The key should be escaped '__proto__'
    // this can be problematic in older engines
    object[k] = v;
  }
  return object;
}
function objectToStringMap(object) {
  let strMap = new Map();
  for (let j of Object.keys(object)) {
    strMap.set(j, object[j]);
  }
  return strMap;
}
```

The above two functions can then be used as follows:

```
  function stringMapToJson(strMap) {
    return
JSON.stringify(stringMapToObject(strMap));
  }
  function jsonToStrMap(jsonStr) {
    return objectToStrMap(JSON.parse(jsonStr));
  }
```

Now that we have the necessary helper functions, we can choose to convert to JSON. This is shown below:

```
  function stringMapToJson(strMap) {
    return
JSON.stringify(stringMapToObject(strMap));
  }
  function jsonToStrMap(jsonStr) {
    return objectToStrMap(JSON.parse(jsonStr));
```

```
}
```

The following example demonstrates how the functions can be used:

```
> let ourMap = new Map().set('yes', true).set('no', false);
> stringMapToJson(ourMap)
'{"yes":true,"no":false}'
> jsonToStrMap('{"yes":true,"no":false}');
Map {'yes' => true, 'no' => false}
```

At this point, you should be aware of how to do the conversion. Very simple and straight forward.

JSON to AMP Format

If you have your content formatted in JSON, it is possible for you to render it in AMP format.

Begin by installing the “article-json-to-amp” into your local machine. Achieve this by executing the following command:

```
npm install article-json-to-amp
```

The following code can then be used for converting the JSON content into an AMP format:

```
const conversion = require('article-json-to-amp');
const myContent = [
 {
  type: 'paragraph',
  children: [
   {
```

```
      type: 'text',
      content: 'This is our text having'
    },
    {
      type: 'text',
      bold: true,
      content: 'a bold text '
    },
    {
      type: 'text',
      href: 'http://sample.com',
      content: 'a link'
    }
  ]
},
{
  type: 'embed',
  embedType: 'image',
  src: 'http://sample/image.jpg',
  width: 300,
```

```
  height: 150
 }
];

console.log(conversion(myContent));
```

Once you execute the above code, you should get the following as the output:

```
<article>
  <p>This is our text
having<b>a bold text </b><a href="http://sample.com
">a link</a></p>
  <figure>
   <amp-
img width="300" height="150" layout="responsive" src=
"http://sample/image.jpg"></amp-img>
  </figure>
</article>
```

HTML to JSON

With the use of "**html-to-article-json," we can parse and then normalize some HTML** so as to get well-structured **content formatted in JSON format.**

Use npm to install this. Just execute the following on the command line:

```
npm install html-to-article-json
```

In node.js, this can be used as demonstrated below:

```
var htmlToJson = require('html-to-article-
json')(opts);

var htmlContent = '<p>Example<b>one</b></p>';

var articleJson = htmlToJson(htmlContent);
```

In the above example, we have created a variable named "htmlToJson" and this will make use of the "html-to-article-json" library which we have just installed. The HTML content which is to be formatted into JSON has been placed in the variable "htmlContent." This variable has then been passed to our initial variable which makes use of the library, and the conversion will be done.

When we use browserify html-to-article-json, we will be in a position to use DOM as the input to our browser. This is shown below:

```
var htmlToJson = require('html-to-article-
json')(opts);
var domElement = document.querySelector('article');
var articleJson = htmlToJson(domElement);
```

In the above example, the variable “htmlToJson” will make use of the library which we have installed. Our DOM element was defined by use of the “domElement” variable. This was then passed to the previous variable for conversion to JSON.

The article-json is made up of a number of nodes, and each of these nodes is used as a representation of a block of content. Consider the example text node given below:

```
{
 "type": "paragraph",
 "children": [{
  "type": "text",
  "content": "Hi, ",
  "href": null,
  "italic": false,
  "bold": false
 },{
  "type": "text",
  "content": "mysite.com",
```

```
    "href": "http://www.mysite.com",
    "italic": true,
    "bold": false
  }]
}
```

In the above code, we have shown how a text node can be defined. When it comes to the representation of text content node, its visual representation is used more than the code.

Embeds

We can also choose to embed some other content inside our code. An example of an embed is video content from YouTube. Consider the example given below demonstrating how this can be done:

```
{
  "type": "embed",
  "embedType": "youtube",
```

```
 "youtubeId": "eCXFOJxYz3W",
 "caption": [{
  "type": "text",
  "content": "This video is from ",
  "href": null,
  "italic": false,
  "bold": false
 },{
  "type": "text",
  "content": "mysite.com",
  "href": "http://www.mysite.com",
  "italic": true,
  "bold": false
 }]
}
```

That is how a YouTube embed can be made.

Chapter 2- Storage and Retrieval of Data in Python with JSON

In Python, you may need to need to represent your data in JSON format. This can simply be done by calling the "json.dumps" function. This can be done as shown in the following example:

```
import json
object = {u"answer": [31.2], u"abs": 31}
print(json.dumps(object))
# output:  {"answer": [31.2], "abs": 31}
```

In most cases, you will need to writing to a network stream or to a file. In Python, you just have to call the "dump" function so as to do this. However, in the later versions of Python, the output to be obtained has to be in the form of a character stream, but in the earlier versions of Python, a byte stream is expected.

It is good for you to know how you can load what you have written. To do this, we make use of the "loads" function when we need to loading from a string, and the "load" function when we need to load from a stream. This is shown below:

```
import json
object_json = u'{"answer": [31.2], "abs": 31}'
object = json.loads(object_json)
print(repr(object))
```

}

Once the loaded and stored objects become too large, one will need to know the starting point of a sub-object. If you need to get this, you have to pass an indent size. This is shown in the code given below:

```
import json
object = {u"answer": [31.2], u"abs": 31}
print(json.dumps(object, indent=4))
```

With the above, you will get a very pretty output as shown below:

```
{
  "abs": 31,
  "answer": [
    31.2
  ]
}
```

Such an indentation feature is of great importance, especially when you need to debug some complex data. Also, it is good for you to know that in Python, it is impossible for you to store some arbitrary Python objects. You have to note that only the following objects can be stored in Python:

- character strings
- booleans (True/False)
- None
- lists
- numbers
- dictionaries having character string keys

If you use an object which is not part of the above, then a conversion has to be done, including objects which belong to the custom class. Consider the following example in which we have an object named "john":

```
class User(object):
    def __init__(self, name, password):
        self.name = name
        self.password = password
john = User('John A. Paul', 'secret')
```

Below is a demonstration of conversion of the above object into JSON and the error that we get:

```
>>> import json
>>> json.dumps(json)
Traceback (most recent call last):
  File "<stdin>", line 1, in <module>
  File "/usr/lib/python3.3/json/__init__.py", line 236, in dumps
    return _default_encoder.encode(object)
  File "/usr/lib/python3.3/json/encoder.py", line 191, in encode
    chunks = self.iterencode(o, _one_shot=True)
```

```
 File "/usr/lib/python3.3/json/encoder.py", line 249, in iterencode
   return _iterencode(o, 0)
 File "/usr/lib/python3.3/json/encoder.py", line 173, in default
   raise TypeError(repr(o) + " is not JSON serializable")
TypeError: <__main__.User object at 0x7f2eccd86551> is not JSON serializable
```

Note that we have passed our object "john" in the dump function. The error clearly shows that the above is not possible. However, there is an escape path. You can implement it just by implementing a default method. This is shown below:

```
def jdefault(o):
   return o.__dict__
print(json.dumps(john, default=jdefault))
# outputs: {"password": "secret", "name": "John A. Paul"}
```

The "o.__dict__" represents some simple catch-all for some user-defined objects, but support for some other objects can also be added. If we need to add some support for the sets, we just have to treat them as lists. This is demonstrated in the code given below:

```
def jdefault(o):
    if isinstance(o, set):
        return list(o)
    return o.__dict__

animals = set([u'Lion', u'Buffalo', u'Elephant'])
print(json.dumps(animals, default=jdefault))
# outputs: ["Lion", "Buffalo", "Elephant"]
```

Chapter 3- The Model-View-Controller (MVC)

It is possible for you to show your JSON output on Spring MVC. The tools to be used in this chapter include the following:

- Eclipse 3.6
- Spring 3.2.2.RELEASE
- JDK 1.6
- Jackson 1.9.10
- Maven 3

Dependencies for the Project

Begin by ensuring that you get the dependencies for both Jackson and Spring. These are explained below:

pom.xml

```
<project xmlns="http://maven.apache.org/POM/4.0.0"
    xmlns:xsi="http://www.w3.org/2001/XMLSchema-
instance"
        xsi:schemaLocation="http://maven.apache.org/POM
/4.0.0
    http://maven.apache.org/maven-v4_0_0.xsd">
        <modelVersion>4.0.0</modelVersion>
        <groupId>com.myenterprise.common</groupId
>
        <artifactId>SpringMVC</artifactId>
        <packaging>war</packaging>
        <version>1.0-SNAPSHOT</version>
        <name>SpringMVC in a Json Webapp</name>
        <url>http://maven.apache.org</url>

        <properties>

        <spring.version>3.2.2.RELEASE</spring.version>
```

```
        <jackson.version>1.9.10</jackson.version>
        <jdk.version>1.6</jdk.version>
    </properties>

    <dependencies>

        <!-- Spring 3 dependencies -->
        <dependency>

            <groupId>org.springframework</groupId>
            <artifactId>spring-core</artifactId>

            <version>${spring.version}</version>
        </dependency>

        <dependency>

            <groupId>org.springframework</groupId>
```

```
<artifactId>spring-web</artifactId>
<version>${spring.version}</version>
</dependency>

<dependency>
<groupId>org.springframework</groupId>
<artifactId>spring-webmvc</artifactId>
<version>${spring.version}</version>
</dependency>

<!-- Jackson JSON Mapper -->
<dependency>
<groupId>org.codehaus.jackson</groupId>
```

```
                    <artifactId>jackson-mapper-
asl</artifactId>

        <version>${jackson.version}</version>
            </dependency>

        </dependencies>

        <build>
            <finalName>SpringMVC</finalName>
            <plugins>
              <plugin>

        <groupId>org.apache.maven.plugins</groupId>
                    <artifactId>maven-eclipse-
plugin</artifactId>
                    <version>2.9</version>
                    <configuration>

        <downloadSources>true</downloadSources>
```

```
<downloadJavadocs>false</downloadJavadocs>

<wtpversion>2.0</wtpversion>
                </configuration>
            </plugin>
            <plugin>

<groupId>org.apache.maven.plugins</groupId>
                <artifactId>maven-compiler-
plugin</artifactId>
                <version>2.3.2</version>
                <configuration>

<source>${jdk.version}</source>

<target>${jdk.version}</target>
                </configuration>
            </plugin>
        </plugins>
```

</build>

</project>

The Model

We will create a simple project in this section, and this will be output as an object which has been formatted in JSON data. In case you need to define some setter and getter methods, you can do it here. This is shown below:

```
package com.myenterprise.common.model;

public class Enterprise {

        String name;
        String memberName[];
//add getter and setter methods here if any
}
```

The Controller

The annotation "@ResponseBody" should be added as the return value. The Spring expects the following:

- The Jackson library readily set in the classpath for the project.
- The annotation "mvc:annotation-driven" readily enabled.
- The Return method readily annotated by use of "@ResponseBody."

If the Spring finds all the above settings ready, the conversion to JSON will be done automatically. The controller class should have the following code:

JSONController.java:

```
package com.myenterprise.common.controller;

import org.springframework.web.bind.annotation.PathVariable;

import org.springframework.web.bind.annotation.RequestMethod;

import org.springframework.web.bind.annotation.RequestMapping;

import org.springframework.web.bind.annotation.ResponseBody;

import org.springframework.stereotype.Controller;

@Controller

@RequestMapping("/kfc/brands")

public class JSONController {
```

```
@RequestMapping(value="{name}", method =
RequestMethod.GET)

public @ResponseBody Enterprise
getEnterpriseInJSON(@PathVariable String name) {

        Enterprise enterprise = new Enterprise();

        enterprise.setName(name);

        enterprise.setStaffName(new
String[]{"myenterprise1", " myenterprise1"});

        return enterprise;

    }

}
```

In the next step, we should enable the property "mvc:annotation-driven" in our XML configuration file for the Spring. This is shown in the code given below:

mvc-dispatcher-servlet.xml:

<beans
xmlns=**http://www.springframework.org/schema/beans**

xmlns:context=**http://www.springframework.org/schema/context**

xmlns:mvc=**http://www.springframework.org/schema/mvc**

xmlns:xsi=**http://www.w3.org/2001/XMLSchema-instance**

xsi:schemaLocation="

http://www.springframework.org/schema/beans

http://www.springframework.org/schema/beans/spring-beans-3.0.xsd

http://www.springframework.org/schema/context

http://www.springframework.org/schema/context/spring-context-3.0.xsd

http://www.springframework.org/schema/mvc

http://www.springframework.org/schema/mvc/spring-mvc-3.0.xsd">

```
        <context:component-scan base-
package="com.mysite.common.controller" />

        <mvc:annotation-driven />


</beans>
```

After that, you will be done. You just have to open it on the browser, and you will get the output. That means that JSON supports the use of the model-view-controller model.

Chapter 4- JSON Web Service

Dart apps working on the client-side need to have a way to communicate with the server. It is recommended that you send JSON in the form of XMLHttpRequest as a way for achieving this. In this chapter, we will show you how to use the HttpRequest API so as to communicate with the server. The data will be from dart:html while the parsing of the JSON data is done using the dart:convert library. You will also be guided on how to use the JsonObject for accessing JSON data by use of the dot notation.

The JSON Web Service

In the majority of modern web applications, the RESTful API is being used and the data under exchange is encoded in JSON format. In this example, we will create a web service which will be responding to a HTTP GET request to a particular URL. The return will be a JSON string, and this will have a string, a list, and a map which will be representing information about the Dart language. This is shown below:

```
{
 "language": "dart",                    // a String
 "targets": ["dartium","javascript"],          // a List
 "website": {                      // a Map
  "homepage": "www.mysite.com",
  "api": "api.mysite.com"
 }
}
```

This web service will also accept data on a similar URL and a HTTP request. Any POST will be interpreted as a request, so that a new object can be created on the server side such as SQL INSERT.

Connection to Server

The HttpRequest API which is provided in the dart:html library provides us with a standard way that we can send and receive data from a web server.

Obtaining the Data from the Web Server

You can use the HTTP GET so as to get objects from the server. The HttpRequest provides us with a constructor named "get" which will take a URL and some callback function which will be invoked once the server has responded. This is shown in the following example:

```
void loadData() {
  var url = "http://127.0.0.1:8080/preferrable -
languages";

  // calling the web server in an asynchronous manner
  var request =
HttpRequest.getString(url).then(onDataLoaded);
}
```

Note that our HTTP Request will be leading to the above URL, that is, http://127.0.0.1:8080/preferrable -languages.

The “onLoadData()” callback can be defined somewhere else in the code, and the “loadData()” function called. This is shown below:

```
// show the raw json response text from your server
void onDataLoaded(String resText) {
  var jsonString = resText;
  print(jsonString);
}

main() {
  loadData();
}
```

The “HttpRequest.getString()” is just a static method which will be used for wrapping the full HttpRequest API. If you need to exercise some full control over your API, you can make use of the full HttpRequest.

Saving the Objects

If you need to vreate a new object on the server side, you can make use of the full HttpRequest API together with the HTTP Post method. The readyStateChange listener should be used, and this will be notified when the request becomes complete. In the example given below, once the request is complete, the onSuccess() method will be called. Here is the code:

```
void saveData() {
  HttpRequest request = new HttpRequest(); //
creating some new XHR
  // adding an event handler which will be called once
the request completes
  request.onReadyStateChange.listen((_) {
   if (request.readyState == HttpRequest.DONE &&
     (request.status == 200 || request.status == 0)) {
    // data was saved saved successfully.
    print(request.resText); // output response from
our server
   }
```

```
 });

 // POST data to our server
 var url = "http://127.0.0.1:8080/preferable-languages";
 request.open("POST", url, async: false);

 String jsonData = '{"language":"dart"}';
 request.send(jsonData); // do an async POST
}
```

Note that a response of 200 shows that we were successful, in that the data was successfully saved to the server.

Parsing the JSON

Now you are aware of how HttpRequest can be used for getting data from server to client, and the data will be posted from the client back to the server. We need to demonstrate how the JSON data can be used in the client application.

The library dart:convert provides us with a JSON class which can be used for the purpose of converting some simple types such as list, int, map, num, and string automatically to and from a JSON string. The two main static methods which can be used for this purpose are the JSON.decode(string) and JSON.encode(object).

When the JSON.decode() function is used, it converts some string having some JSON formatted text into some list of values or some map composed of some key-value pairs, and this is determined by the JSON content.

This is demonstrated in the following example:

```
import 'dart:convert';
main() {
  String listInJson = '["Dart",1.0]'; // input the List of
your data'
  List parsedList = JSON.decode(listInJson);
```

```
 print(parsedList[0]); // Dart

 print(parsedList[1]); // 1.0


 String mapAsJson = '{"language":"dart"}';  // input
Map of data

 Map parsedMap = JSON.decode(mapAsJson);

 print(parsedMap["language"]); // dart

}
```

Note that we are parsing a list of data, and this has been named “listInJson.”

It is also possible for us to make use of JSON when dealing with some complex data structures. Examples of such are the maps nested within lists.

The function JSON.decode() can be used for the purpose of converting the raw Response of HttpRequest to the actual Dart map object. This is shown below:

```
void onDataLoaded(HttpRequest request) {

  Map data = JSON.decode(request.responseText); //
parsing the response //text

  print(data["language"]); // dart

  print(data["targets"][0]);

  print(data["website"]["homepage"]); //
www.mysite.com
}
```

The static method "encode()" will work in the same way as the "decode()" method, but in the reverse manner. This is demonstrated below:

```
void saveData() {

  // snip the setting up HttpRequest

  var mapData = new Map();

  mapData["language"] = "dart";

  mapData["targets"] = new List();

  mapData["targets"].add("dartium");
```

```
String jsonData = JSON.encode(mapData); //
converting the map to String

request.send(jsonData); // performing an async
POST

}
```

When simple maps are used with the strings as the keys, there are some side effects. When a typo is made in the string names, a null value will be returned, and this may cause an error of type “NoSuchMethodError.” For the values to be accessed from the map, it will be impossible for you to validate them before runtime.

When Dart is used, static types are supported. With the static types, it will be possible for you to catch any bugs as early as possible, as any type of mismatches will even be detected before you can run the code, and once a runtime issue has occurred, then an exception will be thrown. When using static types in a IDE and advanced text editors, then there will be auto-completion, making it easy for you to write the code. This is also good for you when the data structure or library you are using is new to you.

It is always good to access the JSON data in a manner which is structured, as with this, you can make use of tools so as to catch any bugs as early as possible. Consider the following Dart code which looks to be more natural:

```
var data = // ... initializing the data ...

// property access has been validated by the tools
print(data.language);
print(data.targets[0]);
```

```
data.website.forEach((key, value) =>
print("$key=$value"));
```

The good thing is that Dart is in support of data access via the dot notation. The best solution is to combine the use of the structure of a class and the flexibility exhibited by a map.

The JsonObject

With the use of the JsonObject, it is easy for one to experience the flexibility of maps and the structure of amps. JsonObject is just a third party library, and it is open source, meaning that one can download and use it for free. JsonObject uses the function named "dart:convert decode()" for extraction of JSON data into a map. The Dart class feature named "noSuchMethod" is then used for the purpose of providing access to the values provided in the map which has been parsed, and this is done by use of the dot notation.

When the noSuchMethod feature is used in JsonObject, it will be in a position to intercept any method calls which are not known. Consider the following example, which demonstrates how we can use a JsonObject instead of using a rawMap:

```
void onDataLoaded(HttpRequest request) {

// decoding the JSON response text by use of
JsonObject
```

```
  JsonObject data = new
JsonObject.fromJsonString(request.responseText);


  // access using dot notation property

  print(data.language);       // Getting some simple
value

  data.language = "Dart";      // Setting some simple
value

  print(data.targets[0]);      // Getting some value from
a list

  // iterate website map

  data.website.forEach((key, value) =>
print("$key=$value"));

}
```

It is also possible for you to use the above together with the classes you have created.

In the following example, we demonstrate how one can factor constructors and implement some interfaces. Here is the code for the example:

```
/// Abstract class is used for defining an interface for our JSON data ///structure

abstract class Language {

  String language;

  List targets;

  Map website;

}


/// Implementation class should extend the JsonObject, and use its ///structure

/// we implement it by creating a Language abstract class.

/// The noSuchMethod() function of JsonObject will provide the actual ///underlying implementation.

class LanguageImplement extends JsonObject implements Language {

  LanguageImplement();


  factory LanguageImplement.fromJsonString(string)

{

    return new JsonObject.fromJsonString(string, new LanguageImplement());
```

```
 }
}
```

It is also possible for you to use such a structure and then implement some string typing on the JSON data. This is shown below:

```
void onDataLoaded(HttpRequest request) {
  // Decoding the JSON response text by use of
LanguageImplement
  // The Language interface will provide the structure
  Language data = new
LanguageImplemnt.fromJsonString(request.resText)
;

  //accessing using the dot notation property
  print(data.language);       // Getting some simple
value
  data.language = "Dart";     // Setting some simple
value
  print(data.targets[0]);     // Getting some value in
the list
  // iterating the map for the website
```

```
data.website.forEach((key, value) =>
print("$key=$value"));

}
```

Note that we have used the class “LanguageImplement” which we have created so as to decode the JSON response text. The structure in this case has been provided by the Language interface. The dot notation has been combined with the instance of the Language for the purpose of access.

With JsonObject, one can easily create a new and empty object, and they will not be expected to first convert this into a JSON string, and this is done by use of a default constructor. This is shown in the following code:

```
var data = new JsonObject();

data.language = "Dart";

data.targets = new List();

data.targets.add("Dartium");
```

It is also possible for us to use the JsonObject for the purpose of implementation of a Map interface, meaning that we will be capable of making use of the normal map syntax. The following code demonstrates how this can be done:

```
var data = new JsonObject();
data["language"] = "Dart"; // the normal map syntax
```

Since JsonObject is used for the purpose of implementing a map, JsonObject can be passed into the JSON.encode() function, and with that, the Map will be converted into JSON so that the data can be sent back to the server. This is shown in the code given below:

```
var data = new
JsonObject.fromJsonString(request.resText);

// converting the JsonObject data back into a string
String json = JSON.encode(data);

// and then POST it back to our server
```

```
HttpRequest request = new HttpRequest();
request.open("POST", url);
request.send(json);
```

JsonObject can be included in the project by use of the "pub" package manager. Your work is just to specify some dependency on the json_object. This is shown below:

```
dependencies:
 json_object: ^1.0.19
```

and then use the import statement given below so as to import the package into the project:

```
import 'package:json_object/json_object.dart';
```

CORS and HttpRequest

It is always good for you to ensure that the app is being served from a single origin just like the web service we are trying to access by use of HttpRequest. The single origin in this case includes the domain name, and the port, as well as the application layer protocol.

JSONP is also another way that one can get the GET request to work, and this involves making some JavaScript callbacks. The interop library for Dart- and JavaScript is "js interop package." This can be used as demonstrated below:

```
import 'dart:html';
import 'package:js/js.dart' as js;

void main() {
 js.scoped(() {
 // creating some top-level JavaScript function named
ourJsonpCallback

   js.context.ourJsonpCallback = new
js.Callback.once( (jsonData) {
```

```
    print(jsonData); // js.Proxy object with the data

  });

  // adding some script tag for api required which is
required
  ScriptElement script = new Element.tag("script");
  // adding some callback function name to our URL
  script.src =
"http://sample.com/some/api?callback=ourJsonpCal
lback";
  document.body.children.add(script); // adding
some script to the DOM
 });
}
```

Chapter 5- XML and JSON Views

JsonView and XmlView can be used for the purpose of creating both JSON and XML responses. This can then be integrated with "Cake\Controller\Component\RequestHandlerComponent."

Once the "RequestHandlerComponent" has been enabled in the application, and support for xml or json extensions is enabled, it becomes easy for us to leverage the new classes.

Data views can be generated in two main ways. In one of the ways, we make use of the "_serialize" key and in the second way; we just create normal template files.

How to Enable Data Views in an App

Before using the data view classes, the "Cake\Controller\Component\RequestHandlerComponent" should first be loaded into the controller. This can be done as shown below:

```
public function initialize()
{
  ...
  $this->loadComponent('RequestHandler');
}
```

You can choose to do this in the AppController, and automatic view class switching will be automatically enabled on the content types. The component can also be setup in the setting for "viewClassMap," and this will enable the mapping of types to the custom classes or map other data types.

The xml or json extensions can also be enabled as an option with the Routing File Extensions. With that, we will be in a position to access JSON, XML, or some other views with a special format, and we will use some custom URL ending having a name of the response type ending being the extension for the file.

In case the Routing File Extensions is not enabled, the Accept header wills use for specifying the type of format which will be displayed to the user.

Data View and Serialize Key

The _serialize key is just a special view variable which is used for the purpose of indicating the other view variable which is to be serialized when we are using a data view. With this, the step for creation of template files for the controller actions can be skipped if you don't need to do any action format before conversion of the data into json/xml format.

If there is a need for some formatting or manipulation to be done on the view variables before generation of the response, you can just make use of template files. The value for the _serialize can take either an array of view variables which are to be serialized or a string. This is shown below:

```
namespace App\Controller;
class OurController extends AppController
{
  public function initialize()
  {
    parent::initialize();
    $this->loadComponent('RequestHandler');
  }

  public function index()
  {
    // Setting the vars for the view which are to be serialized.
```

```
    $this->set('articles', $this->paginate());
    // Indicating the view vars JsonView has to serialize.
    $this->set('_serialize', ['articles']);
  }
}
```

The _serialize can also be defined as an array having some view variables to be combined. This is demonstrated below:

```
namespace App\Controller;

class OurController extends AppController
{
  public function initialize()
  {
    parent::initialize();
    $this->loadComponent('RequestHandler');
  }
```

```
public function index()
{
    // Part of code which created the $articles and the $comments

    // Setting the vars for view which are to be serialized.
    $this->set(compact('articles', 'comments'));

    // Indicating the view vars JsonView has to serialize.
    $this->set('_serialize', ['articles', 'comments']);
}
}
```

When the _serialize is defined as an array, we get an added advantage in that a top level <response> element will be appended once the xmlview is being used.

If the value for XmlView and _serialize is a string, it is good for you to ensure that the view variable will have a single top-level element. If no top-level single element exists, then the XML will not be generated.

Data View and Template Files

The template files should be used when you need to perform some of the view content before the final output can be created. Consider a situation where a field has generated some HTML in your content. In such a case, you may need to omit this in the JSON response. A view file would be very essential in such a situation:

```
//Code for the controller
class OurController extends AppController
{
  public function index()
  {
    $articles = $this->paginate('Articles');
    $this->set(compact('articles'));
  }
}
```

```
// View the code -
src/Template/Articles/json/index.ctp

foreach ($articles as &$$article) {

  unset($article->generated_html);

}

echo json_encode(compact('articles'));
```

It is possible for you to perform some manipulations which are more complex, as well as make use of helpers so as to do the formatting. The data view classes will not support the layouts. Their assumption is that the serialized content will be output in the view file.

Chapter 6- Android and JSON

In Android, there are the android.org libraries which make it easy to work with the JSON files. It is also possible for you to include the libraries which you can use to parse the JSON files. We need to demonstrate how these libraries can be used in Android.

Create a new Android project. Give the project the name

"COM.NMS.MYPROJECT.JSON," *THE* PACKAGE THE NAME "COM.NMS.NYPROJECT.JSON," AND THE ACTIVITY THE NAME "PARSEMYPROJECTACTIVITY."

Open the activity, and then add the following code to it. Our aim is to download the Twitter feed for the user with the name “nms,” and the number of entries together with the text messages will be sent or written to a text file. This is shown below:

```
package com.nms.android.myproject.json;

import java.io.IOException;
import java.io.InputStream;
import org.apache.http.HttpResponse;
import java.io.InputStreamReader;

import org.apache.http.HttpEntity;
import org.apache.http.client.methods.HttpGet;
import org.apache.http.StatusLine;
import java.io.BufferedReader;
import
org.apache.http.client.ClientProtocolException;
import android.os.Bundle;
```

```
import
org.apache.http.impl.client.DefaultHttpClient;
import org.apache.http.client.HttpClient;
import org.json.JSONObject;
import org.json.JSONArray;
import android.app.Activity;
import android.util.Log;

public class ParseMyProjectActivity extends Activity {
    /** will be called once the activity is created for the first
time. */
    @Override
    public void onCreate(Bundle savedInstanceState)
{
        super.onCreate(savedInstanceState);

        # Allowing for network access in main thread
for testing purposes
        # DON'T use this in a productive code
```

```
        StrictMode.ThreadPolicy policy = new
StrictMode.
        ThreadPolicy.Builder().permitAll().build();
        StrictMode.setThreadPolicy(policy);

        setContentView(R.layout.main);
        String input = readNms();
        try {
            JSONObject json = new
JSONObject(input);

Log.i(ParseMyProjectActivity.class.getName(),
jsonObject.toString());
            }
        } catch (Exception e) {
            e.printStackTrace();
        }
    }

    public String readBugzilla() {
```

```
        StringBuilder builder = new StringBuilder();
        HttpClient client = new DefaultHttpClient();
        HttpGet httpGet = new HttpGet(

"https://nms.mozilla.org/rest/bug?assigned_to=nico
hsam@mozilla.com");

        try {
            HttpResponse response =
client.execute(httpGet);
            StatusLine statusLine =
response.getStatusLine();
            int statusCode =
statusLine.getStatusCode();
            if (statusCode == 200) {
                HttpEntity entity =
response.getEntity();
                InputStream content =
entity.getContent();
                BufferedReader reader = new
BufferedReader(
```

```
                                new
InputStreamReader(content));
                    String line;
                    while ((line = reader.readLine()) !=
null) {
                        builder.append(line);
                    }
                } else {
                    Log.e(ParseJSON.class.toString(),
"The file was not downloaded");
                }
            } catch (ClientProtocolException ex) {
                ex.printStackTrace();
            } catch (IOException ex) {
                ex.printStackTrace();
            }
            return builder.toString();
        }
}
```

Before running the code, ensure that you have opened the ANdroidManifest.xml file and then added the permission for “android.permission.INTERNET.” The process of writing JSON is also very easy. You just have to create a JSONObject or some JSONArray, and then make use of the “toString()” method. This is shown in the following code:

```
public void writeJSON() {
    JSONObject obj = new JSONObject();
    try {
        obj.put("name", "John Joel");
        obj.put("score", new Integer(150));
        obj.put("current", new Double(213.32));
        obj.put("nickname", "Boss");
    } catch (JSONException ex) {
        ex.printStackTrace();
    }
    System.out.println(obj);
}
```

Chapter 7- JSON and Go

When using the JSONpackage, it becomes easy for you to read and write your data from Go programs.

The "marshal" function is used for encoding the JSON data. This can be used as shown below:

```
func Marshal(v interface{}) ([]byte, error)
```

Consider the Go data structure named "Message" as shown below:

```
type Message struct {
   Name string
   Body string
   Time int64
}
```

We also have an instance of the Message as shown below:

m := Message{"John", "Hi", 23767063945815210000}

We can then make use of the "json.Marshal" so as to marshal some JSON-encoded version of the instance m. This is shown below:

b, err := json.Marshal(m)

If the above command runs successfully, the "err" will just be a nil, while the "b" will just be a []byte having the JSON data.

Decoding

The "Unmarshal" function is used when we need to decode our JSON data. The function can be used as shown below:

func Unmarshal(data []byte, v interface{}) error

Let us create some space in which the storage of the decoded data will be done. This can be done as follows:

var m Message

After that, we can call the json.Unmarshall() function by passing some []byte of the JSON data and some pointer to m.

This is shown below:

err := json.Unmarshal(b, &m)

If the JSON data for b is valid and can fit in m,

Conclusion

We have come to the end of this book. My hope is that you have learned how to use JSON. Conversions can easily be done in Python. It is possible for us to convert strings into JSON objects, and the vice versa is true. Note that we use JSON for the purpose of rendering data on web pages. We can take a JSON object and then convert it into the corresponding JavaScript notation. We can also use the GSON object, which can help work with both JSON and Java.

This tool will help us convert our code and objects from Java to JSON. The vice versa is true, as we can use the same tool to convert from JSON to Java. In Python, we can use the JSON for the purpose of retrieving the data that we need. JSON also supports the use of the Model-View-Controller model. My hope is that you are good in using this as it has been discussed in this book.

JSON is highly versatile, and we can combine it with the other programming languages so as to get some amazing apps. Both XML and JSON can be combined for creation of amazing views.

Printed in Great Britain
by Amazon